flowers the essencial touch

contents

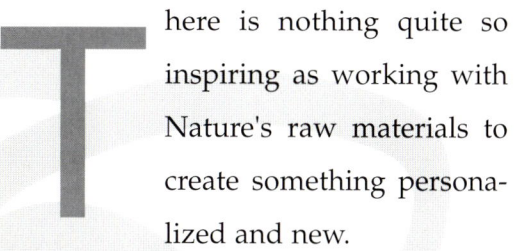

There is nothing quite so inspiring as working with Nature's raw materials to create something personalized and new.

With just a handful of basic ingredients –plants, flowers (the earth's natural works of art) and perhaps some colorful ribbon and wire– you can effortlessly create fantastic floral arrangements to suit any mood you wish to convey: an air of mystery, a streak of playfulness or a classic, refined atmosphere.

In deciding upon the myriad of floral arrangements possible, we have chosen a variety of styles, all of which are surprisingly simple to put together. We hope that, once you are familiarized with these basic ingredients, you feel free to branch off in new directions, perhaps joining elements from different centerpieces. In short, we hope that you feel inspired by our designs and that, above all, you have fun with them!

centerpiece

Type of composition: Decortive with stand. Table composition.
Materials used: Two-tier stand, rose, Easter lily, turban buttercup, asparagus, trumpet vine, copper wire, hyacinth, Gloriosa rotschildiana, Saint-john's-wort, platycladus, galax, laurustinus, moss, cyclamen leaves.

Working from the base of the stand, decorate the top tier with loose elements, incorporating a supply of water for the flowers. At the bottom, insert the stems directly into the foam. Always leave enough space to ensure that the line of sight of those seated at the table is not blocked.

1 2 3 4 5 6 7 8

compositions

centerpieces

Style: Creative
Technique: Mixed
Color scheme: Contrasting
Size: 60 cm. diameter
Tendency: Clustered

This is a very creative decoration due to the variety of materials that make up the whole. First, cut some branches of box shrub into rounded shapes and arrange them in old earthenware flowerpots on top of a wooden board covered with decorative leaves. These are accompanied with fresh cushions of natural moss. A point of contrast is provided by overturned flowerpots spilling out delicate cascades of white flowers. Fruit supplies dashes of color in perfect harmony with the various clusters.

Ingredients

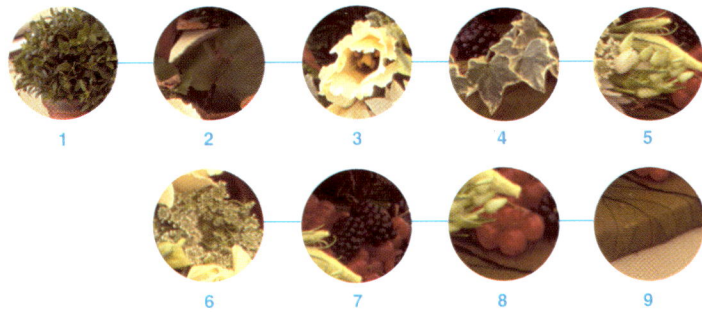

1. Buxus sempervirens / Boj   2. Galax aphylla / Galax   3. Eustoma grandiflora / Eustoma
4. Hedera helix / English ivy   5. Ornithogalum narbonense pyramidale / Ornithogalum   6. Ammi majus / Ammi
7. Blackberries   8. Ribes rubrum / Redcurrants   9. Bahuinia grandiflora / Bahuinia

centerpieces

Style: Radial asymmetric decorative
Technique : Foam
Color scheme: Ranging from pink to violet
Size: For a table 120 cm in diameter
Tendency: Mixed

Arrangement with two complementary elements on a circular surface. As this quite large table is set for two, the decoration must create an intimate space. Start assembling the piece by creating a broad base with the greenery. With such a large base the central force is obtained by using a heavy color, capable of offsetting the height. Build the base up, working around as you go to create perfect chromatic harmony on all sides.

🌹 Ingredients

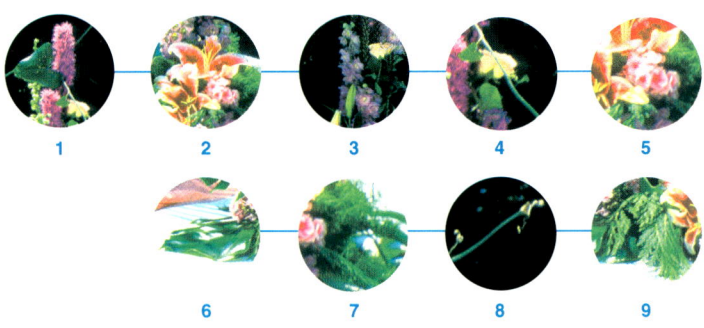

1. Liatris spicata / Liatris 2. Lilium Star Gaze / Lily 3. Consolida ambigua / Rocket larkspur
4. Rosa Vivaldi / Rose 5. Phlox hortorum / Phlox 6. Monstera deliciosa / Swiss cheese plant
7. Asparagus umbellatus midiocladus / Asparagus 8. Smilax aspera / Sarsaparilla
9. Platycladus orientalis / Platycladus

Style: Loose formal
Technique: Foam
Color scheme: Harmonious
Size: 25 cm. diameter
Tendency: Units

This arrangement appears loose purely as a result of the leaves, which are kept low so as not to create a barrier between the fellow diners. The anthurium flower and the glass bulb containing a candle lend the composition an elegant tone. The same centerpiece is used to decorate the entrance to the dining room, thus creating a uniform effect.

Ingredients

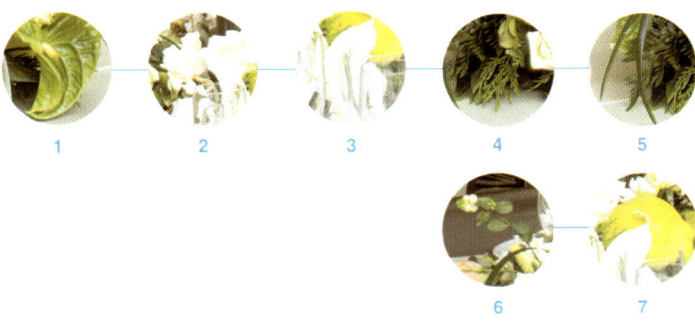

1 2 3 4 5

6 7

1.Anthurium midori / Anthurium 2.Eustoma grandiflora / Eustoma 3.Lilium Casablanca / Lily

4.Polystichum coriaceum / Holly fern 5.Ophiopogon jaburan / Ophiopogon 6.Hydrangea macrphylla /

French hydrangea 7.Quinces

centerpieces

Style: Classic linear
Technique : Foam
Color scheme: Contrasting
Size: 50x50 cm.
Tendency: Units

The two sides of the "L" are well balanced, forming a perfect right angle, the vertex of which is intensified with a bold splash of color. If the work were restricted to these two lines the result would be a strong optical bias towards the right, avoided in this case by the visual impact of the Swiss cheese plant leaf. This also provides color contrast and dictates the intensely formal character of the piece.

Ingredients

1 2 3 4 5

6

1. Protea repens / Protea 2. Gerbera jamesonii / Gerbera 3. Monstera deliciosa / Swiss cheese plant
4. Eucalyptus spiralus baby / Eucalyptus 5. African greenery 6. African greenery

centerpieces

Style: Horizontal parallel
Technique: Units
Color scheme: Contrasting
Size: 100x100 cm.
Tendency: Clustered

The color contrast of the decoration as a whole underlines the clarity of definition of the parallel formed by the reeds and bird-of-paradise leaves. Both the orange of the gerbera and the splayed shape of the cold, clean-textured bird-of-paradise flower contrast with the balls of moss, creating a perfect balance of forms. This visually pleasing centerpiece can be arranged directly on the tablecloth without the need of a support or base.

Ingredients

1. Strelitzia reginae / Bird-of-paradise flower   2. Gerbera tenesi / Gerbera   3. Consolida ambigua / Rocket larkspur
4. Arundo donax / Giant reed   5. Strelitzia reginae / Bird-of-paradise flower   6. Galax aphylla / Galax
7. Actinidia chinensis / Kiwi fruit (stem)   8. Asparagus falcatus / Asparagus   9. Balls of moss

centerpieces

Style: Directional
Technique: Submerged
Color scheme: Contrasting
Size: 40x40 cm.
Tendency: Structure

This piece should be made in a clear glass container that will enhance its effect and blend in with the surface below. Place a small wreath of wisteria vine into the container and use it as a base for weaving all the materials into a circular shape, the flowers and the greenery thus creating a sort of nest. All the materials should be very supple. If any of them are too stiff (this may be the case with the stem of the umbrella plant), work them with the hands until they are pliable. The rose in the middle adds a touch of romanticism.

Ingredients

1

2

3

4

5

6

7

1. Ornithogalum narbonense pyramidale / Ornithogalum   2. Phormium tenax / Fornio, New Zeland hemp
3. Achillea Lilac Beauty / Yarrow   4. Cyperus alternifolius / Umbrella plant   5. Rosa Ruby / Rose
6. Zinnia elegans / Zinnia   7. Asparagus sprengeri / Asparagus

centerpieces

Style: Formal linear
Technique: Foam
Color scheme: Yellow and complementary
Size: 110 cm. diameter
Tendency: Experimental

To decorate this table, it was first draped with sack cloth reaching down to the floor in regular pleats. The tablecloth is a somewhat softer tarlatan in contrasting tones (blues and lilacs). The originally shaped plates and the simplicity of the handles of the cutlery, made of tied cinnamon sticks, and the individual bread baskets –flowerpots wrapped in raffia– make the whole scene delightful.

 **Ingredients**

1   2   3   4   5

1.Gerbera jamesonii / Gerbera   2.Ammi majus / Ammi   3.Hedera helix / English ivy (fruits)
4.Hazelnuts   5.Raffia (natual and dyed)

centerpieces

Style: Loose asymmetric decorative
Technique: Foam
Color scheme: Harmony in pinks
Size: 100x120 cm.
Tendency: Clustered

This piece is specifically designed to be placed at one end of a head table, where its loose lines can be appreciated to the full. The arrangement is worked around the radius and branches out in many directions. Candles can be added, depending on the occasion. The form is rather atypical for a table arrangement and less spectacular than is traditionally the case, yet its singularity produces some striking effects.

Ingredients

    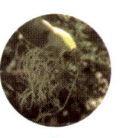

1   2   3   4   5

1 Lilium Star Gaze / Lily   2 Gerbera mini / Gerbera (miniature)   3 Ampelopsis tricuspicata / Boston ivy
4 Celosia pyramidalis / Celosia   5 Clematis vitalba / Traveller's joy

centerpieces

Style: Linear wth structure
Technique: Foam
Color scheme: Contrasting
Size: Height 50 cm.
Tendency: Clustered

A combination of structure and composition arranged in linear clusters. The main part consists of a cluster grouped around a metal structure, the horizontal lines of which offset the verticality of proportions 5 and 3. The elegance and sophistication of velvet contrasts with the rustic, metallic texture of the structure.

Ingredients

1. Gerbera jamesonii / Gerbera   2. Rosa champagnella / Rose (champagne-colored)
3. Galax aphylla / Galax   4. Liatris spicata / Liatris   5. Achillea filipendulina / Yarrow
6. Monstera deliciosa / Swiss cheese plant   7. Asparagus sprengeri / Asparagus
8. Prunus laurocerasus / Cherry laurel   9. Molucella laevis / Shell flower
10. Salix matsudana tortuosa / Contorted willow   11. Platycladus orientalis / platycladus
12. Typha latifolia / Common cattail   13. Asparagus plumosus / Asparagus fern
14. Asparagus falcatus / Asparagus

centerpieces

Style: Buffet decoration
Technique: Foam
Color scheme: Monochrome and complementary
Size: 50x30 cm.
Tendency: Clustered

Originality in the choice of greenery and its unusual placing, seeking maximum asymmetry while maintaining a very regular base, is the key to interpreting this composition, which is rich in textures and color, shape and definition. Tranquility and balance surround the palm fruits, thus lightening their overall effect.

Ingredients

1. Cordyline terminalis / Ti 2. Platycladus orientalis / Platycladus 3. Polystichum coriaceum / Holly fern
4. Helianthus annus var. macrophyllus / Sunflower (without petals) 5. Agapathus africanus / African lily
6. Ananas comosus / Pineapple 7. Palm fruits 8. Musgo polar / Moss (treated)
9. Gaultheria shallon / Salal 10. Gerbera jamesonii / Gerbera 11. Achillea filipendulina / Yarrow

centerpieces

Style: Buffete decoration
Technique: Foam
Color scheme: Polychrome
Size: 150x70 cm.

A buffet decoration in two parts with complementary color schemes; one part consists of flowers and the other fruit. Good positioning is the key to their successful distribution, reinforced by particular emphasis on the central axis. The callas give light and dynamism to the nighttime background, etching the profile of the composition.

Ingredients

1. Rosa Tina / Rose (orange) 2. Protea repens / Protea 3. Zantedeschia aethiopica / Common florist's calla 4. Paeonia lactiflora / Chinese peony 5. Hedera helix / English ivy 6. Cyperus alternifolius / Umbrella plant 7. Polystichum coriaceum / Holly fern 8. Platystemon leicocarpus / Platyspermum 9. Grapes 10. Bananas 11. Apples (green and red) 12. Oranges 13. Pineapple

centerpieces

Style: Decorative
Technique: Foam
Color scheme: Harmonious
Size: 80x40x40 cm.
Tendency: Clustered

Fruits and vegetables are used to represent the warm, bountiful autumn, together with sharply etched branches in harmonious colors and a great wealth of elements. A contrasting echo of the centerpiece is placed on one side, causing a complementary visual impact and adding linear agility to the composition.

Ingredients

1. Cydonia oblonga / Quince   2. Platycladus orientalis / Platycladus   3. Salix matsudana tortuosa / Contorted willow
4. Bouganvillea glabra / Bouganvillea   5. Chestnut   6. Sweet potato   7. Pomegranate   8. Pear   9. Quince

centerpieces

Style: Decorative
Technique: Foam
Color scheme: Contrasting
Size: 40x40 cm.
Tendency: Clustered

Ideal centerpiece for dinner parties. For its warm, sunny tones and the choice of vegetation used, the composition is a symbolic representation of Mediterranean cuisine. The centerpiece is constructed on a low base, first placing the candle in the center and then arranging all the materials (the volumes of which will be proportional to the size of the candle) along the radius, making sure that the color is balanced on all sides.

Ingredients

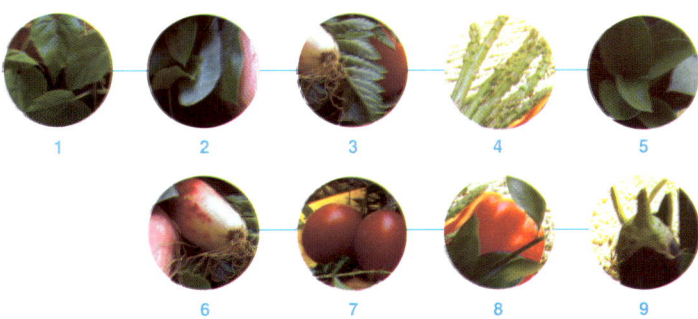

1. Parthenocissus tricuspidata / Boston ivy 2. Eucalyptus globulus / Cider gum
3. Polystichum coriaceum / Holly fern 4. Asparagus shoots 5. Ruscus hypoglossum / Butcher's broom
6. Shallots 7. Tomatoes (on the stalk) 8. Peppers 9. Egg plant

centerpieces

Style: Buffet decoration
Technique: Foam
Color scheme: Contrasting
Size: 30 cm. diameter
Tendency: Clustered

It is essential to have access to a good quality rustic basket. Inside this, place a well-secured block of foam and line it completely with cabbage leaves, so that the foam does not come into direct contact with the vegetables. The alter are arranged in clusters, focusing the interest and giving touches of light with the white elements. Any materials that might shift should be wired.

Ingredients

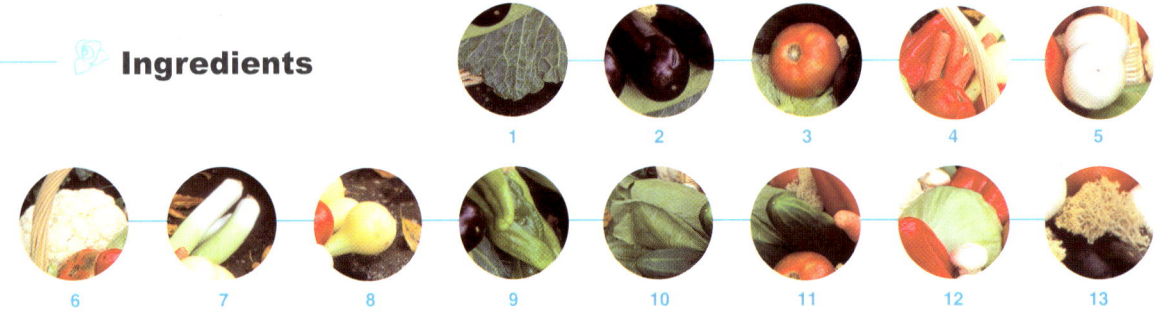

1   2   3   4   5

6   7   8   9   10   11   12   13

1. Cabbage leaves 2. Egg plant 3. Tomatoes 4. Carrots 5. Mushrooms 6. Cauliflower 7. Leaks 8. Shallots
9. Peppers (green and red) 10. Lettuce 11. Cucumber 12. Summer cabbage 13. Moss (treated)

centerpieces

Style: Formal symmetric decorative
Technique: Foam
Color scheme: Range of yellows
Size: 70x40 cm.
Tendency: Clustered

Once you have chosen the basket, insert blocks of dry foam, making sure that they are well attached to the base. Then distribute the materials in clusters, in such a way that the highest part is in the middle. Note the loops of esparto string that crown the loaf in the center. All the elements are rustic, with a countrified feel, and are reminiscent of a warm, sunny rural setting.

Ingredients

1. Rosa golden times / Rose (golden)   2. Pinus nigra / Black pine   3. Eucalyptus ochre / Eucalyptus (dyed)
4. Triticum durum / Durum wheat   5. Achillea filipendulina / yarrow   6. Helycrisum arenarium / Inmortelle
7. Lavanda latifolia / lavender

centerpieces

Style: Buffet decoration
Technique: Foam
Color scheme: Polychrome
Size: 1.70 m. x 85 cm.
Tendency: Baroque still life

The mixture of spiky, multidirectional, round and spherical shapes of the fruits, together with compact placement and a variety of warm reds and yellows, crafts a style close to the baroque. The bottom of the composition has to hold considerable weight, and should therefore be lined with a plastic or wire mesh to avoid it splitting.

Ingredients

1. Anthurium Green Peace / Anthurium 2. Chrysanthemum indicum hibrido Spider / Chrysanthemum 3. Rosa Vicky Braun / Rose (two-colored) 4. Lilium hollandicum / Lily 5. Liatris spicata / Liatris 6. Mostera deliciosa / Swiss cheese plant 7. Fatsia japonica / Fatsia 8. Aspidistra elatior / Aspidistra 9. Chrysanthemum Statesman / Chrysanthemum 10. Apples 11. Bananas 12. Cauliflower

centerpieces

Style: Vertical formal
Technique: Foam
Color scheme: Harmonious
Size: 120x 80 cm.
Tendency: Units

The center of the work is complemented with greenery, plaited esparto cord and flowering garlic to lend it greater force. Once the foam is in place, insert the flowers to mark out the principal points, fixing the height, depth and base without going beyond the triangle they describe. The flowering garlic is a risky choice, as it is more straightforward to work with spiky or mixed flowers. Nevertheless, the result here is entirely convincing.

Ingredients

1   2   3   4   5

6   7   8

Allium giganteum / Flowering garlic   Rosa Vivaldi / Rose   Lilium Star Gaze / Lily
Polystichum coriaceum / Holly fern   Chamaedorea elegans / Chamadorea
Braided esparto cord   Eucalyptus globulus / Cider gum   Sparto grass

centerpieces

Style: Formal asymmetric
Technique: Foam
Color scheme: Complete range
Size: 40x50 cm.
Tendency: Textural

Textural arrangements provide their surroundings with an overwhelming amount of elements that are rich on their own and when grouped together acquire great expressive strength. The starting point is the asymmetric axis of the roses, which is also the basis for the distribution of textures, forms and color, yielding an end result with a symmetric form.

Ingredients

1. Phylodendron augustisectum / Philodendron   2. Nephrolepis exaltata / Sword fern   3. Prunus laurocerasus / Cherry laurel   4. Rosa Vicky Braun / Rose (two-colored)   5. Asparagus falcatus / Asparagus   6. Achillea Lilac Beauty / Yarrow   7. Polystichum coriaceum / Holly fern   8. Achillea filipendulina / Yarrow   9. Eustoma grandiflora / Eustoma   10. Limonium sinuatum / Limonium   11. Aster novi-belgii / Aster (lilac)   12. Callistephus chinensis / China aster   13. Hypericum balearicum / Saint-john's-wort (fruits)   14. Salix viminalis / Common osier   15. Rosa skimo / Rose (white)

centerpieces

Style: Linear horizontal
Technique: Structure
Color scheme: White
Size: 150x40 cm.
Tendency: Transparency

First attach the foam to the mouth of the container, since the curve of the structure exerts a lot of pressure and could easily lift it out. The structure is made by tying the wicker with raffia, thus fixing it and maintaining the desired shape. Then cover the base with the greenery, taking into account that the core of the piece is bunched and the rest complementary, with the raised part forming a transparency.

Ingredients

1. Prunus laurocerasus / Cherry laurel 2. Platycladus orientalis / Platycladus 3. Campsis radicans / Trumpet vine
4. Asparagus sprengeri / Asparagus 5. Molucella laevis / Shell flower 6. Hypericum balearicum / Saint-john's-wort (fruits)
7. Solidago canadensis / Canadian goldenrod 8. Rose (two-colored) 9. Dianthus caryophyllus / Carnation
10. Lilium longiflorum / Easter lily 11. Salix viminalis / Common osier

centerpieces

Style: Decorative asymmetric
Technique: Foam
Color scheme: Monochrome
Size: 80x40 cm.
Tendency: Enveloping

A decorative composition that is balanced by the positioning of the greenery. The verticality of the arrangement is its great strength. When making it, be sure to combine very different green materials, as regards both shape and texture, in an inverse proportion (the less flowers used, the greater their importance). The positioning and the enveloping form of the New Zealand hemp leaves create an optical interplay between the elements in the foreground and those that can be glimpsed in the back.

Ingredients

1   2   3   4   5

Rosa Dallas / Rose (red) Phormium tenax / New Zeland hemp Cyperus alternifolius / Umbrella plant
Fatsia japonica / Fatsia Asparagus meyeri / Asparagus

centerpieces

Style: Decorative parallel
Technique: Foam
Color scheme: Monochrome
Size: 50x30 cm.
Tendency: Mixed

A parallel arrangement that uses different heights to obtain a decorative structure. This result is achieved by choosing a multidirectional type of base flower. The main cluster is eclipsed by a richer arrangement at the base. The size of the gerbera and its concentric nature dictate the limits of the composition, which is notable for its homogeneity of tones, offset by the interesting note of complementary color.

Ingredients

1.Platycladus orientalis / Platycladus   2.Gerbera jamesonii / Gerbera   3.Chrysanthemum coronarium / Chrysanthemum
4.Lilium Connecticut King / Lily   5.Phormium tenax / New Zeland hemp   6.Limonium sinuatum / Limonium
7.Raffia   8.Polystichum híbrido / Holly fern   9.Howea belmoreana / Paradise plant (leaves)   10.Glass candles
11.Ornithogalum caudatum / Ornithogalum

centerpieces

Style: Decorative
Technique: Spiral
Color scheme: Contrast
Size: 60x35 cm.
Tendency: Transparency

An intensely worked form of bouquet, thoroughly integrated with its base. It displays an interplay of transparencies of fresh, natural color, making a sober, simple arrangement. The choice of flowers and the hazel that are used in conjunction with the coconut palm fiber limit the composition to the winter months; the arrangement is a harbinger of spring bursting forth, represented symbolically by the spider plant and the cyrtomium leaves. Water is supplied through a plastic tube, which means that the bouquet can also be used as centerpiece or a sideboard arrangement.

Ingredients

1. Rosa Motrea / Rose (red) 2. Aster dumosus / Áster (white) 3. Cyrtomium falcatum / Cyrtomium
4. Chlorophytum comosum / Spider plant 5. Corylus avellana / Hazelnut
6. Cortaderia selloana / Pampas grass 7. Coconut fiber

centerpieces

Style: Decorative semispherical
Technique: Organic
Color scheme: Harmonious triad
Size: 35 cm. diameter
Tendency: Units

The support for this composition is a woven wicker structure held in place by the overhanging lip of the base itself, which contains water. Reinforce the wicker structure, once woven, with sarsaparrilla vine. Then insert the greenery and flowers, ensuring that their stalks can reach the water. The organic structure gives the composition a modern feel, which contrasts with the classical style of the semispherical form.

Ingredients

1. Salix viminalis / Common osier 2. Smilax aspera / Sarsaparrilla 3. Galax aphylla / Galax
4. Asparagus umbellatus midiocladus / Asparagus 5. Rosa porcelina multiflora / Rose (profusely flowering)
6. Zinnia elegans / Zinnia 7. Ageratum houstonianum / Ageratum

centerpieces

Style: Formal
Technique: Spiral
Color scheme: Contrast
Size: 50x40 cm.
Tendency: Structured

The idea inspiring this bouquet is to make a structure in straw and let everything pass through and over it, as occurs in nature when dead and green plants mingle in the same landscape. Without sacrificing order and taste to form, the elements are arranged with striking naturalness. Soft, round, elegant forms in juxtaposition with fresh green tones help to underline its natural character.

🌸 Ingredients

1

2

3

4

5

6

1. Tulipa gesnerana / Tulip   2. Syringa vulgaris / Common lilac   3. Viburnum opulus / Guelder rose
4. Hedera helix / English ivy   5. Euphorbia fulgens / Scarlet plume   6. Straw structure

centerpieces

Style: Formal
Technique: Foam
Color scheme: Yellow and complementary
Size: 60x40 cm.
Tendency: Clusters

The positioning of most of the flowers is active, in contrast with the passiveness of the love-lies-bleeding. It establishes an interplay of lines and shapes that are balanced in themselves, despite deceptive appearances to the contrary. With its overwhelmingly summery tones, the composition boasts both elegant and rustic elements, although the nature of the base inclines it more towards the alter flower. The glow of the lighter hue matches the maroons and lilacs perfectly.

Ingredients

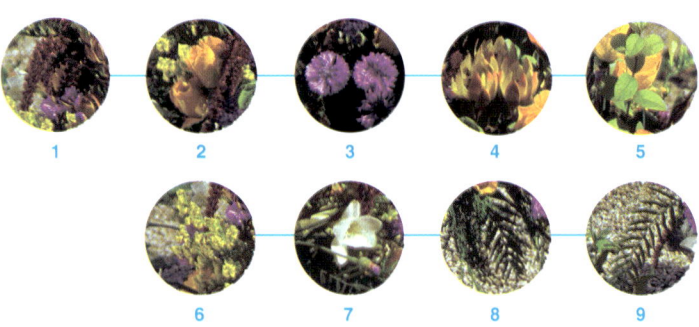

1   2   3   4   5

6   7   8   9

Amaranthus caudatus / Love-lies-bleeding   Rosa Tina / Rose (orange)
Centaurea cyanus / Cornflower   Leucadendron safari sunset / Silver tree
Ligustrum ovalifolium variegatum / California privet (variegated)   Solidago canadensis /
Canadian goldenrod   Freesia hibrida / Freesia   Platycladus orientalis / Platycladus
Schinus molle / Pepper tree

christmas

centerpieces

Style: Classical
Technique: Foam
Color scheme: Contrasting
Size: 35 cm. diameter
Tendency: Clustered

The groups of red candles are the keynotes in this Christmas arrangement, laid out in an 8-5-3 ratio on a bed of elegant green leaves whose sober, quiet shape transforms this centerpiece into a festive classic without recourse to the ubiquitous Christmas tree. At the foot of each group of candles anthurium leaves are used to create a graphic, enveloping line.

Ingredients

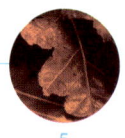

1

2

3

4

5

6

1.Cymbidium Gy Cooksbridge / Cybidium 2.Spathiphyllum kochii / Peace lily 3.Platycladus orientalis / Platycladus
4.Anthurium veitchii / Anthurium 5.Quercus robur / English oak 6.Polystichum coriaceum / Holly fern

centerpieces

Style: Classical / Formal
Technique : Foam
Color scheme: Contrasting
Size: 35 cm. diameter
Tendency: Bunched

The festive nature of this piece is shown by the candle, the balls and the curls, while the artificial fruits and dried hydrangeas add wintry connotations. With its somber materials, warm colors and simple form and finish, this centerpiece is not difficult to make, and yet represents an essential element of Christmas decoration.

 **Ingredients**

1 2 3 4

1. Abies procera / Noble fir   2. Hydrangea macrophylla / French hydrangea   3. Decorative curls
4. Red christmas balls

centerpieces

Style: Parallel
Technique : Foam
Color scheme: Neutral
Size: 20 x 15 cm
Tendency: Units

A simple arrangement in cool colors, with base and candle in blue. Going unnoticed, avoiding glances, the will not to attract the attention of those present, is the expression of a piece containing a few simple elements. Each one of these elements manages to maintain a space and a character of its own: the moss with its cushion-like feel, and the pine cones with their gentle chiaroscuro.

Ingredients

1 2 3 4

Musgo polar / Moss (treated)   Pine cones   Lichen   Candle

centerpieces

Style: Linear
Technique: Foam
Color scheme: Blue, burgundy and pink
Size: 50 cm. diameter
Tendency: Textural with flourish

The circular base is divided by an asymmetric bough, the starting point around which the clusters are arranged in an 8-5-3 ratio to break the monotony. The hardness of the bough and pine cones is mitigated by their interaction with soft pink and blue tones, in perfect harmony with the satiny texture of the base. The white stars with gold glitter, attached with coiled wire, provide a Christmas touch.

Ingredients

1. Chrysanthemum Kloindike / Chysanthemum (burgundy) 2. Hedera helix / English ivy 3. Rosa gerdo / Rose
4. Centaurea cyanus / Cornflower 5. Asparagus umbellatus midiocladus / Asparagus 6. Bough 7. Pine cones

centerpieces

Style: Formal
Technique: Foam
Color scheme: Contrasting
Size: 80x35 cm.
Tendency: Semitransparency

Using the most traditional of materials in classical forms with a semitransparent tendency, we obtain a centerpiece with a modern feel. A touch of gold on the edges of the rose petals adds a hint of sophistication to the whole, at the same time countering the rustic notes of the fir and the lichen on the branches.

Ingredients

    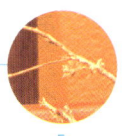

1   2   3   4   5

1. Rosa pareo / Orange rose   2. Rosa Dallas / Red rose   3. Ilex aquifolium / Holly
4. Abies procera / Noble fir   5. Lichen

centerpieces

Style: Formal
Technique: Foam
Color scheme: Monochrome
Size: 40 cm. diameter
Tendency: Units

This centerpiece is made out of the sort of things you might come across on a walk in the country or round a garden, and its merit lies in the way the various homogenous materials have been put together. The whole arrangement seems to have been conceived with one purpose: to recreate the coziness of wintertime. It is charged with vitality and aroma by small eucalyptus blooms, which at the same time are redolent of winter.

Ingredients

1 2 3 4 5

1. Spruce cone   2. Asparagus umbellatus midiocladus / Asparagus   3. Abies procera / Noble fir
4. Platycladus orientalis / Platycladus   5. Eucalyptus globolus / Cider gum (in bloom)

centerpieces

Style: Formal
Technique: Collage
Color scheme: Warm
Size: 40x36 cm.
Tendency: Clustered

The contrast between the transparency of the decorative fabric on its rustic wreath and the irregular side cluster makes for an exquisite duality. The luxury expressed by the transparency transports one to a festive atmosphere, an elegant, sumptuous dinner followed by champagne. The compact core centers the work and provides it with a specific optical weight.

Ingredients

   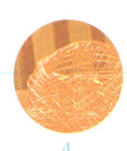 

1.Abies procera / Noble fir   2.Magnolia soulangiana / Saucer magnolia (leaves)   3.Wicker wreath
4.Mesh fabric   5.Christmas balls   6.Paper bows

centerpieces

Style: Free
Technique: Organic structure
Color scheme: Chromatic
Size: 70x30 cm.
Tendency: Clustered

Make a wicker structure and attach it to the base with lengths of raffia. Everything is woven or tied together or suspended in such a way as to be completely stable. Whereas some of the materials are quite independent, others wrap gently round each other, creating an interplay of lines that sets the rhythms of the piece.

Ingredients

1　2　3　4　5

6

1.Salix viminalis / Common osier 2.Maranta leuconeura / Prayer plant 3.Rosa canina / Dog rose
4.Yucca gloriosa / Spanish dagger 5.Tulipa gesnerana / Tulip 6.Pine cones

centerpieces

Style: Decorative
Technique: Dry foam
Color scheme: Contrasting
Size: 60x48x35 cm.
Tendency: Clustered

Fill a wickerwork base to the brim with foam, ensuring that no gap is left in the middle, otherwise it will be difficult to keep the candles completely vertical. Once the central axis is properly established, mark the two ends with platycladus and corncobs respectively. Then insert the remaining elements, making sure that they are not excessively bunched. This center-piece is the result of a balanced mixture of elegance and rusticity that can easily be adapted to any surroundings.

Ingredients

Zea mays / Maize (dyed corn cob)   Schinus molle / Pepper tree   Platycladus orientalis / Platycladus
Golden mushroom   Raffia (natural, dyed)   Hazelnuts   Foeniculum vulgare / Fennel

centerpieces

Style: Decorative asymmetric
Technique: Radial
Color scheme: Chromatic
Size: 80x55 cm.
Tendency: Stil life

A still life for Christmas, made entirely out of natural materials of animal and plant origin. It has a rustic feel, the pheasant's elegant plumage providing great chromatic richness, and constituting the common ground between all the elements that make up the composition. Unless the pheasant is a gift, it is advisable to use a stuffed bird. The springs of pepper tree add movement to the center of the still life.

Ingredients

1.Schinus molle / Pepper tree (leaves and fruits)   2.Gerbera jamesonii hibrida / Gerbera

3.Passiflora caerulea / Passion flower   4.Prunus laurocerasus / Cherry laurel   5.Kingfisher

6.Pheasant   7.Pumpkins   8.Quinces

garden

centerpieces

Style: Buffet accessory
Technique: Foam
Color scheme: Monochrome
Size: 150 cm. diameter
Tendency: Units

This arrangement can be made throughout the year, although in this case it takes on a summery feel due to the fragrance of the tuberoses and the striking effect of the shell flower. It is an accessory with can be used to recreate a buffet ambience in the open air, its outdoor location allowing, moreover, the incorporation of perfumed flowers. The very open angles and falling lines, concealing the base and almost touching the water, give the arrangement majesty and radiance.

Ingredients

1 2 3 4 5

6

1. Gladiolus communis / Gladiolus   2. Chrysanthemum Reagan / Chysanthemum
3. Molucella laevis / Shell flower   4. Polianthes tuberosa / Tuberose
5. Eucalyptus simmondsii / Eucalyptus   6. Hydrangea macrophylla / French hydrangea

centerpieces

Style: Formal
Technique: Foam
Color scheme: contrasting
Size: 75 cm. diameter
Tendency: Clustered

With its clear formal composition, clean-cut brightness and cheery range of colors, this composition represents a crisp, sunny winter's day, a world away from melancholy leaden skies. It is a veritable song to the winter season. In spite of the rustic appearance of the earthenware base, the elegance of the flowers used in the arrangement maintains a sense of balance, making the piece suitable for all styles.

Ingredients

1. Lilium hollandicum / Lilly (yellow and orange) 2. Gerbera jamesonii / Gerbera
3. Gladiolus communis / Gladiolus 4. Hedera helix / English ivy 5. Asparagus spregeri / Asparagus
6. Aster dumosus / Aster (white) 7. Matthiola incana annua / Stocks 8. Aster novibelgii / Aster (lilac)

centerpieces

Style: Buffet accessory
Technique: Compact
Color scheme: Contrasting
Size: Height 120 cm.
Tendency: Clustered

Much of the interest lies in the form of the stand, which facilitates the two-tier composition of the piece in a complementary, agile fashion. Shape is provided by the larger elements, tied on with rushes or attached with florist's hooks. Finish it off with the smaller pieces, at the same time inserting the cut foliage, which helps fill it out.

Ingredients

1. Peppers 2. Egg plant 3. Asparagus densiflorus / Asparagus 4. Leaks
5. Cortaderia selloana / Pampas grass 6. Red cabbage 7. Shallots
8. Ruscus hypoglossum / Butcher's broom 9. Monstera deliciosa / Swiss cheese plant

centerpieces

Style: Vegetative buffet decoration
Technique: Organic
Color scheme: contrasting
Size: 1.30m.x1m.x80cm.
Tendency: Romantic transparency

An old, sun-bleached basket of the sort used by snail gatherers is the starting point for a composition with a simple formal structure. It brings together elements we associate with autumn, highlighting them against a golden background that conjures up an image of ploughed fields. The tenuous light recalls the approach of winter and dreams of vegetation. The loose lines that emerge from the center both upwards and downwards are united by the splash of color at the optical point.

Ingredients

Aloysia triphylla / Lemon verbena   Salix matsudana tortuosa / Contorted willow
Passiflora caerulea / Passion-flower   Ricinus communis / Castor bean
Helianthus annus var. macrophyllus / Sunflower   Zinnia elegans / Zinnia

centerpieces

Style: Decorative
Technique: Foam
Color scheme: Harmonious
Size: 22 cm. diameter
Tendency: Units

Composition arranged by units, making the rhythms more continuous and presenting the table companions with an image that is more pleasing to the eye. The variety of the plants used provides the overall picture with greater richness. The nature of the different elements enable them to complement each other easily, giving rise to flowing creativity without falling into repetitious monotony.

Ingredients

1.Anthurium midori / Anthurium (green) 2.Hydrangea macrophylla / French hydrangea
3.Eustoma grandiflora / Eustoma 4.Symphoricarpos albus / Snowberry 5.Rosa champagnella / Rose
(champagne-colored) 6.Chamaecyparis lawsoniana / Lawson cypress 7.Ophiopogon jaburan / Ophiopogon

centerpieces

Style: Symmetric formal pyramid
Technique: Foam
Color scheme: From pink to lilac
Size: 100x40 cm.
Tendency: Units

The verticality of the central cluster imposes itself over the spherical flowers that adorn the base, thus creating an interplay between them. The parallel central cluster is the starting point, the rings of flowers getting gradually wider around the foam base. Finally, the composition is completed with leaves of holly fern, the color of which adds visual weight to the base.

Ingredients

1   2   3   4   5

6   7   8   9

1. Polystichum coriaceum / Holly fern   2. Callistephus chinensis / China aster
3. Dianthus loretta / Carnation (miniature)   4. Eustoma grandiflora / Eustoma   5. Dianthus caryophyllus / Carnation
6. Gerbera jamesonii / Gerbera   7. Liatris spicata / Liatrix   8. Chrysanthemum "cassa" / Chrysanthemum
9. Gladiolus communis / Gladiolus

Editor
Josep Mª Minguet

Production and Art Director
Louis Bou

Graphic Design and Layout
Mònica Pera

Documentation and Writing
Flora Miserachs

Photography
Joan Argelés

Links International
c/ Jonqueres, 10. 1º, 5ª
08003 Barcelona
Tel. +34 93 301 21 99
Fax:+34 93 301 00 21

info@linksbooks.net
www.linksbooks.net

© I.Monsa de Ediciones,S.A.

ISBN: 84-89861-17-X
DL: B-12438 -2003
Printed in Spain

epu.l
Edições e Publicações, Lda
Telef: 213 161 192 Fax: 213 161 194
e-mail: epu.l@epu.l.mail.pt
Rua José Falcão, nº 57 - 4º Esq.
1000-184 Lisboa - Portugal